This journal belongs to

....

Date

....

*A*mazing grace! How sweet the sound
That saved a wretch like me!
I once was lost, but now am found;
Was blind, but now I see.

JOHN NEWTON

*F*or it is by grace you have been saved,
through faith—and this not from yourselves,
it is the gift of God—not by works,
so that no one can boast.

EPHESIANS 2:8–9 NIV

ntroduction

You are a beloved child of God, precious to Him in every way.
He cares about you and knows the desires of your heart.
Since your first breath, He has been writing His
amazing grace into the story of your life.

Be inspired by the words of the classic hymn "Amazing Grace"
as you pen your own story on these pages. Let God weave
His story into yours, unfolding His unique plans for you
and deepening your faith. With contemporary writings and
Scripture, *Amazing Grace* is a place to express your thoughts,
record your prayers, and discover God's tender love for you.

May His peace guide your heart always.
And may His amazing grace become the defining
theme of your story, your faith, and your life.

Grace is something you can never get but can only be given.
There's no way to earn it or deserve it or bring it about
anymore than you can deserve the taste of raspberries and cream.
A good night's sleep is grace and so are good dreams.
Most tears are grace. The smell of rain is grace.
Somebody loving you is grace.

FREDERICK BUECHNER

For God saved us and called us to live a holy life. He did this, not because we deserved it, but because that was his plan from before the beginning of time—to show us his grace through Christ Jesus.

2 TIMOTHY 1:9 NLT

*Not that we deserve it, not that we can earn it,
but that we know how precious and valuable a gift it is.
That's what makes grace so amazing!*

From his fullness we have all received, grace upon grace.

JOHN 1:16 ESV

How else do we accept His free gift of salvation if not with thanksgiving? Thanksgiving is the evidence of our acceptance of what He gives. Thanksgiving is the manifestation of our Yes to His grace.

ANN VOSKAMP

_I_ will give you thanks, for you answered me;
you have become my salvation.

PSALM 118:21 NIV

*Grace comes free of charge to people who do not deserve it,
and I am one of those people.... Now I am trying
in my own small way to pipe the tune of grace.*

PHILIP YANCEY

Since we have been justified through faith, we have peace with God through our Lord Jesus Christ, through whom we have gained access by faith into this grace in which we now stand.

ROMANS 5:1–2 NIV

Not only are we saved by grace, we live by it as well.

RICHARD J. FOSTER

God is able to make all grace abound to you, so that...in all things
at all times, you may abound in every good work.

2 CORINTHIANS 9:8 ESV

The entire life of following Jesus is only possible by the grace of God. It all starts and ends with Him.

MICHAEL NEALE

I am the Alpha and the Omega—the Beginning and the End. To all
who are thirsty I will give freely from the springs of the water of life.

*Unreasonable grace! Nothing is reasonable
about the love of God or the gifts He so freely gives!*

BETH MOORE

The LORD God is a sun and shield; the LORD will give grace and glory;
no good thing will He withhold from those who walk uprightly.

PSALM 84:11 NKJV

God is looking for people who will come in simple dependence upon His grace and rest in simple faith upon His greatness. At this very moment, He's looking at you.

JACK HAYFORD

....

....

....

....

....

....

....

....

....

....

....

....

....

....

*O*nly in returning to me and resting in me will you be saved.
In quietness and confidence is your strength.

ISAIAH 30:15 NLT

*G*race comes into the soul as the morning sun into the world;
first a dawning, then a light, and at last the sun
in his full and excellent brightness.

THOMAS ADAMS

May God give you more and more grace and peace as you
grow in your knowledge of God and Jesus our Lord.

2 PETER 1:2 NLT

'Twas grace that taught my heart to fear,
And grace my fears relieved;
How precious did that grace appear,
The hour I first believed!

JOHN NEWTON

*F*or the grace of God has appeared, bringing salvation for all people, training us to renounce ungodliness and worldly passions, and to live self-controlled, upright, and godly lives in the present age.

TITUS 2:11–12 ESV

In whatever ways that the Lord is blessing you...
I hope that you will recognize His winsome ways.
He customizes every dream He places in our hearts.

ROBIN JONES GUNN

You have found grace in My sight,
and I know you by name.

EXODUS 33:17 NKJV

Don't we all long for a father...who cares for us in spite of our failures? We do have that type of a father. A father who is at His best when we are at our worst...whose grace is strongest when our devotion is weakest.

MAX LUCADO

This is your Father you are dealing with, and he knows better than you what you need. With a God like this loving you, you can pray very simply.

MATTHEW 6:7–8 MSG

God wants us to approach life, full of expectancy that [He] is going to be at work in every situation as we release our faith in Him.

COLIN URQUHART

*W*e can rejoice, too, when we run into problems and trials,
for we know that they help us develop endurance.
And endurance develops strength of character, and character
strengthens our confident hope of salvation.

ROMANS 5:3–4 NLT

It is not objective proof of God's existence that we want but the experience of God's presence. That is the miracle we are really after, and that is also, I think, the miracle that we really get.

FREDERICK BUECHNER

....

....

....

....

....

....

....

....

....

....

....

....

....

*God's Spirit touches our spirits and confirms
who we really are. We know who he is,
and we know who we are: Father and children.*

ROMANS 8:16 MSG

If you believe in God, it is not too difficult to believe that He is concerned about the universe and all the events on this earth. But the really staggering message of the Bible is that this same God cares deeply about you and your identity and the events of your life.

BRUCE LARSON

When you're in over your head, I'll be there with you. When you're in rough waters, you will not go down. When you're between a rock and a hard place, it won't be a dead end—because I am GOD, your personal God, the Holy of Israel, your Savior. I paid a huge price for you...! *That's* how much you mean to me! *That's* how much I love you!

ISAIAH 43:2–4 MSG

Emptiness itself can birth the fullness of grace because in the emptiness we have the opportunity to turn to God, the only begetter of Grace, and there find all the fullness of joy, peace, rest.

ANN VOSKAMP

May the God of hope fill you with all joy and peace
as you trust in him, so that you may overflow with hope
by the power of the Holy Spirit.

ROMANS 15:13 NIV

Be assured, if you walk with Him and look to Him
and expect help from Him, He will never fail you.

GEORGE MUELLER

The LORD always keeps his promises;
he is gracious in all he does.

PSALM 145:13 NLT

Faith isn't the ability to believe long and far into the misty future. It's simply taking God at His word and taking the next step.

JONI EARECKSON TADA

*Trust in the Lord with all your heart,
and lean not on your own understanding.*

PROVERBS 3:5 NKJV

Through many dangers, toils, and snares,
I have already come;
'Tis grace has brought me safe thus far,
And grace will lead me home.

JOHN NEWTON

Thus far the LORD has helped us.

1 SAMUEL 7:12 NKJV

Do you believe that God is near? He wants you to. He wants you to know that He is in the midst of your world. Wherever you are as you read these words, He is present. In your car. On the plane. In your office, your bedroom, your den. He's near. And He is more than near. He is active.

MAX LUCADO

*S*urely goodness and love will follow me all the days of my life,
and I will dwell in the house of the LORD forever.

PSALM 23:6 NIV

In our quest for living a pure, focused life that pleases God,
we all hit the wall at one time or another. What do we do then? Give up....
Not an option. I have had times when the road has gotten long....
Those periods can be very challenging. When they happen,
I go to God and ask for His strength for the journey.

REBECCA ST. JAMES

*O*n the inside, where God is making new life,
not a day goes by without his unfolding grace.

2 CORINTHIANS 4:16 MSG

Grace is the central invitation to life and the final word.
It's the beckoning nudge and the overwhelming,
undeserved mercy that urges us to change and grow,
and then gives us the power to pull it off.

TIM HANSEL

....

....

....

....

....

....

....

....

....

....

....

....

....

....

*A*re you tired? Worn out? Burned out on religion? Come to me.
Get away with me and you'll recover your life. I'll show you how
to take a real rest. Walk with me and work with me—
watch how I do it. Learn the unforced rhythms of grace.

MATTHEW 11:28–29 MSG

Comfort and prosperity have never enriched the world
as much as adversity has done. Out of pain and problems have come
the sweetest songs, the most poignant poems, the most gripping stories.
Out of suffering and tears have come the greatest spirits
and the most blessed lives.

BILLY GRAHAM

For you, God, tested us; you refined us like silver....
But you brought us to a place of abundance.

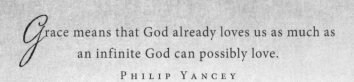

Grace means that God already loves us as much as an infinite God can possibly love.

PHILIP YANCEY

*Your love, LORD, reaches to the heavens,
your faithfulness to the skies.*

PSALM 36:5 NIV

We know that [God] gives us every grace, every abundant grace;
and though we are so weak of ourselves, this grace is able
to carry us through every obstacle and difficulty.

ELIZABETH ANN SETON

The LORD is good, a strong refuge when trouble comes.
He is close to those who trust in him.

NAHUM 1:7 NLT

*Jesus Christ is no security against storms, but He is perfect
security in storms. He has never promised you
an easy passage, only a safe landing.*

L. B. COWMAN

God is our refuge and strength, an ever-present help in trouble.
Therefore we will not fear, though the earth give way
and the mountains fall into the heart of the sea.

PSALM 46:1–2 NIV

When it's beyond our power and strength to make it on our own,
we know beyond certainty that it was God, and not ourselves,
that got us through. He receives greater glory when we are depleted and
cry out to Him for the strength to walk through the hardship.

REBECCA ST. JAMES

He comes alongside us when we go through hard times, and before you know it, he brings us alongside someone else who is going through hard times so that we can be there for that person just as God was there for us.

2 CORINTHIANS 1:4 MSG

We get one story, you and I, and one story alone. God has established the elements, the setting, and the climax and resolution. It would be a crime not to venture out, wouldn't it?

DONALD MILLER

The LORD will fulfill his purpose for me;
your steadfast love, O LORD, endures forever.

PSALM 138:8 ESV

The Lord has promised good to me.
His word my hope secures;
He will my shield and portion be,
As long as life endures.

JOHN NEWTON

God's way is perfect. All the LORD's promises prove true.
He is a shield for all who look to him for protection.

2 SAMUEL 22:31 NLT

*R*emember you are very special to God as His precious child.
He has promised to complete the good work He has begun in you.
As you continue to grow in Him, He will teach you
to be a blessing to others.

GARY SMALLEY AND JOHN TRENT

He who began a good work in you will carry it
on to completion until the day of Christ Jesus.

PHILIPPIANS 1:6 NIV

I could provide a long list of all...the hurts and missteps and conflicts....
But then come the golden moments, and these are the times
when [everyone] must stop and smile and clear the air.... It is here,
in the uncluttered heart, that the Author and Finisher of our faith
writes new songs, new stories, new promises.

ROBIN JONES GUNN

*C*reate in me a clean heart, O God,
and renew a right spirit within me.

PSALM 51:10 ESV

God promises to keep us in the palm of [His] hand, with or without our awareness. God has already made a space for us, even if we have not made a space for God.

DAVID AND BARBARA SORENSEN

Let us hold tightly without wavering to the hope we affirm,
for God can be trusted to keep his promise.

HEBREWS 10:23 NLT

All that we have and are is one of the unique and never-to-be repeated ways God has chosen to express Himself in space and time. Each of us, made in His image and likeness, is yet another promise He has made to the universe that He will continue to love it and care for it.

BRENNAN MANNING

*For we are His workmanship,
created in Christ Jesus for good works.*

EPHESIANS 2:10 NKJV

Some days, it is enough encouragement just to watch the clouds break up and disappear, leaving behind a blue patch of sky and bright sunshine that is so warm upon my face. It's a glimpse of divinity; a kiss from heaven.

May God be gracious to us and bless us
and make his face shine on us.

PSALM 67:1 NIV

*I*ncredible as it may seem, God wants our companionship. He wants to have us close to Him. He wants to be a father to us, to shield us, to protect us, to counsel us, and to guide us in our way through life.

BILLY GRAHAM

*B*ecause we are his children, God has sent the Spirit...into our hearts, prompting us to call out, "Abba, Father."

GALATIANS 4:6 NLT

We think God's love rises and falls with our performance. It doesn't....
He loves you for whose you are: you are His child.

MAX LUCADO

See what great love the Father has lavished on us, that we should be
called children of God! And that is what we are!

1 JOHN 3:1 NIV

God's grace is alive and at work in us. It is not a one-time event but the ever-flowing power at work in us by the Holy Spirit. We stand in grace. We are strengthened by grace. We are encouraged to grow in grace.

MICHAEL NEALE

*G*row in the grace and knowledge of our
Lord and Savior Jesus Christ.

2 PETER 3:18 NIV

*T*he Creator thinks enough of you to have sent Someone
very special so that you might have life—
abundantly, joyfully, completely, and victoriously.

I have come that they may have life,
and that they may have it more abundantly.

JOHN 10:10 NKJV

Grace is not simply leniency when we have sinned.
Grace is the enabling gift of God not to sin.
Grace is power, not just pardon.

JOHN PIPER

May he give you the power to accomplish
all the good things your faith prompts you to do.

2 THESSALONIANS 1:11 NLT

Everything in life is most fundamentally a gift. And you receive it best, and you live it best, by holding it with very open hands.

LEO O'DONOVAN

The fulfillment of God's promise depends entirely on trusting God
and his way, and then simply embracing him and what he does.
God's promise arrives as pure gift.

ROMANS 4:16 MSG

He is the Source. Of everything. Strength for your day.
Wisdom for your task. Comfort for your soul. Grace for your battle.
Provision for each need. Understanding for each failure.
Assistance for every encounter.

JACK HAYFORD

....

....

....

....

....

....

....

....

....

....

....

....

....

*W*hoever drinks the water I give them will never thirst.
Indeed, the water I give them will become in them
a spring of water welling up to eternal life.

JOHN 4:14 NIV

Yes, when this flesh and heart shall fail,
And mortal life shall cease;
I shall profess, within the vail,
A life of joy and peace.

JOHN NEWTON

....

....

....

....

....

....

....

....

....

....

....

....

So let us come boldly to the throne of our gracious God. There we will receive his mercy, and we will find grace to help us when we need it most.

God comforts. He doesn't pity. He picks us up, dries our tears, soothes our fears, and lifts our thoughts beyond the hurt.

ROBERT SCHULLER

*G*od is our merciful Father and the source of all comfort.

2 CORINTHIANS 1:3 NLT

*F*aith in God gives your life a center from which you can reach out and dare to love the world.

BARBARA FARMER

Strength is for service, not status. Each one of us needs to look after the good of the people around us, asking ourselves, "How can I help?"

ROMANS 15:1–2 MSG

A changed life lived for Christ is the greatest proof
to man there is a God—a God who is alive and
working in frail human vessels like ourselves.

CAROLYN LUNN

But we have this treasure in jars of clay to show that this
all-surpassing power is from God and not from us.

Grace tells us that we are accepted just as we are. We may not be the kind of people we want to be... we may have more failures than achievements...we may not even be happy, but we are nonetheless accepted by God, held in His hands.

MCCULLOUGH

We throw open our doors to God and discover at the same moment
that he has already thrown open his door to us. We find ourselves
standing where we always hoped we might stand—
out in the wide open spaces of God's grace and glory.

ROMANS 5:2 MSG

$\mathscr{T}$here is nothing but God's grace. We walk upon it; we breathe it; we live and die by it; it makes the nails and axles of the universe.

ROBERT LOUIS STEVENSON

*T*he Lord longs to be gracious to you;
therefore He will rise up to show you compassion.

Isaiah 30:18 niv

Grace...expresses two complementary thoughts:
God's unmerited favor to us through Christ,
and God's divine assistance to us through the Holy Spirit.

JERRY BRIDGES

Because of his great love for us, God, who is rich in mercy, made us alive with Christ even when we were dead in transgressions— it is by grace you have been saved.

EPHESIANS 2:4–5 NIV

The purpose of grace is primarily to restore our relationship
with God.... The work of grace aims at...an ever deeper
knowledge of God and an ever closer fellowship with Him.
Grace is God drawing us to Himself.

J. I. PACKER

But as for me, the nearness of God is my good; I have made the Lord GOD my refuge, that I may tell of all Your works.

PSALM 73:28 NASB

Hope is definitely not the same thing as optimism. It is not the conviction that something will turn out well, but the certainty that something makes sense, regardless of how it turns out.

VÁCLAV HAVEL

*N*ow faith is confidence in what we hope for
and assurance about what we do not see.

HEBREWS 11:1 NIV

God may be invisible, but He's in touch. You may not be able to see Him, but He is in control. And that includes you—your circumstances. That includes what you've just lost. That includes what you've just gained. That includes all of life—past, present, future.

CHARLES R. SWINDOLL

*W*ho shall separate us from the love of Christ? Shall trouble
or hardship or persecution or famine or nakedness or danger or sword?...
No, in all these things we are more than conquerors
through him who loved us.

ROMANS 8:35, 37 NIV

It is when things go wrong, when good things do not happen, when our prayers seem to have been lost, that God is most present.

MADELEINE L'ENGLE

God's love, though, is ever and always, eternally present to all
who fear him, making everything right for them...
as they follow his Covenant ways.

PSALM 103:17-18 MSG

*T*he grace of God means something like: Here is your life. You might never have been, but you are because the party wouldn't have been complete without you. Here is the world. Beautiful and terrible things will happen. Don't be afraid. I am with you. Nothing can ever separate us. It's for you I created the universe. I love you.

FREDERICK BUECHNER

I am convinced that nothing can ever separate us from God's love.
Neither death nor life, neither angels nor demons,
neither our fears for today nor our worries about tomorrow—
not even the powers of hell can separate us from God's love.

ROMANS 8:38 NLT

The earth shall soon dissolve like snow,
The sun forbear to shine;
But God, who called me here below,
Will be forever mine.

JOHN NEWTON

....

....

....

....

....

....

....

....

....

....

....

....

*G*race, because God is putting everything together again
through the Messiah, invites us into life—
a life that goes on and on and on, world without end.

ROMANS 5:21 MSG

God gets down on His knees among us; gets on our level
and shares Himself with us. He does not reside
afar off and send diplomatic messages, He kneels among us....
God shares Himself generously and graciously.

EUGENE PETERSON

For God so loved the world that he gave his one and only Son,
that whoever believes in him shall not perish but have eternal life.

JOHN 3:16 NIV

God is not really "out there" at all. That restless heart, questioning who you are and why you were created, that quiet voice that keeps calling your name is not just out there, but dwells in you.

DAVID AND BARBARA SORENSEN

It's in Christ that we find out who we are and what we are living for.
Long before we first heard of Christ and got our hopes up,
he had his eye on us, had designs on us for glorious living.

EPHESIANS 1:11 MSG

God loves to look at us, and loves it when we will look back at Him. Even when we try to run away from our troubles...God will find us, bless us, even when we feel most alone.... God will find a way to let us know that He is with us *in this place*, wherever we are.

KATHLEEN NORRIS

You will seek me and find me when
you seek me with all your heart.

Life varies its stories. Time changes everything, yet what is truly valuable—what is worth keeping—is beyond time.

RUTH SENTER

No eye has seen, no ear has heard, and no mind has imagined
what God has prepared for those who love him.

1 CORINTHIANS 2:9 NLT

No created being can ever know how much and how sweetly and tenderly God loves them. It is only with the help of His grace that we are able to persevere in spiritual contemplation with endless wonder at His high, surpassing, immeasurable love which our Lord in His goodness has for us.

JULIAN OF NORWICH

I pray that you, being rooted and established in love,
may have power, together with all the Lord's holy people,
to grasp how wide and long and high and deep is the love of Christ.

EPHESIANS 3:17–18 NIV

With God, life is eternal—both in quality and length. There is no joy comparable to the joy of discovering something new from God, about God. If the continuing life is a life of joy, we will go on discovering, learning.

EUGENIA PRICE

The earth will be filled with the knowledge of the LORD
as the waters cover the sea.

ISAIAH 11:9 NIV

Grace has taken over and drawn me in and I am embracing it
'Cause now I see Your light drawing me close
Overwhelming love I don't deserve.

REBECCA ST. JAMES

For God, who said, "Let light shine out of darkness," made his light shine in our hearts to give us the light of the knowledge of God's glory.

2 CORINTHIANS 4:6 NIV

God wants you to know Him as personally as He knows you.
He craves a genuine relationship with you....
He didn't make us robots, preprogrammed to love Him and follow Him.
He gave us free will and leaves it to us to choose to spend time with Him.
That way it's genuine. That way it's a real relationship.
TOM RICHARDS

It's who you are and the way you live that count before God.
Your worship must engage your spirit in the pursuit of truth.
That's the kind of people the Father is out looking for: those who are
simply and honestly *themselves* before him in their worship.

JOHN 4:23 MSG

The grace of God...there's only one catch. Like any other gift, the gift of grace can be yours only if you'll reach out and take it. Maybe being able to reach out and take it is a gift too.

FREDERICK BUECHNER

The promise is received by faith.
It is given as a free gift.

ROMANS 4:16 NLT

There is an essential connection between experiencing God, loving God, and trusting God. You will trust God only as much as you love Him, and you will love Him to the extent you have touched Him, rather that He has touched you.

BRENNAN MANNING

I will put my laws in their minds and write them on their hearts.
I will be their God, and they will be my people.

HEBREWS 8:10 NIV

What makes life worthwhile is having a big enough objective,
something which catches our imagination and
lays hold of our allegiance.... What higher, more exalted,
and more compelling goal can there be than to know God?

J. I. PACKER

....

....

....

....

....

....

....

....

....

....

....

....

....

....

....

So let us know, let us press on to know the LORD.
His going forth is as certain as the dawn; and He will come to us
like the rain, like the spring rain watering the earth.

HOSEA 6:3 NASB

*G*race is the dynamic outpouring of God's loving nature
that flows into and through creation in an endless
self-offering of healing, love, illumination, and reconciliation.
It is a gift that we are free to ignore, reject, ask for, or simply accept.

GERALD G. MAY

*Because of his grace he declared us righteous
and gave us confidence that we will inherit eternal life.*

TITUS 3:7 NLT

We are always in the presence of God.... There is never a non-sacred moment! His presence never diminishes. Our awareness of His presence may falter, but the reality of His presence never changes.

MAX LUCADO

Whom have I in heaven but you? And earth has nothing
I desire besides you. My flesh and my heart may fail, but God is
the strength of my heart and my portion forever.

PSALM 73:25–26 NIV

When we've been there ten thousand years,
Bright shining as the sun,
We've no less days to sing God's praise
Than when we'd first begun.[†]

You have turned my mourning into joyful dancing...
that I might sing praises to you and not be silent.
O LORD my God, I will give you thanks forever!

PSALM 30:11–12 NLT

Your worst days are never so bad that you are beyond the reach of God's grace. And your best days are never so good that you are beyond the need of God's grace.

JERRY BRIDGES

Show me the wonders of your great love....
Keep me as the apple of your eye;
hide me under the shadow of your wings.

PSALM 17:7–8 NIV

If God wants you to do something, He'll make it possible for you to do it, but the grace He provides comes only with the task and cannot be stockpiled beforehand. We are dependent on Him from hour to hour, and the greater our awareness of this fact, the less likely we are to faint or fail in a crisis.

LOUIS CASSELS

My grace is sufficient for you,
for My strength is made perfect in weakness.

2 CORINTHIANS 12:9 NKJV

As the caterpillar finds its new ability to fly, we should be thrilled over our Spirit-empowered ability to live differently and faithfully. Isn't this what the Scriptures speak of? Isn't this what we've all been longing for?

FRANCIS CHAN

This means that anyone who belongs to Christ has become
a new person. The old life is gone; a new life has begun!
And all of this is a gift from God, who brought us
back to himself through Christ.

2 CORINTHIANS 5:17–18 NLT

The needed change within us is God's work, not ours.
The demand is for an inside job, and only God can work
from the inside. We cannot attain or earn this righteousness
of the kingdom of God: it is a grace that is given.

RICHARD J. FOSTER

*A*ll the while, you will grow as you learn to know God better
and better.... For he has rescued us from the kingdom of darkness
and transferred us into the Kingdom of his dear Son,
who purchased our freedom and forgave our sins.

COLOSSIANS 1:10, 13–14 NLT

The growth of grace is like the polishing of metals. There is first an opaque surface; by and by you see a spark darting out, then a strong light; till at length it sends back a perfect image of the sun that shines upon it.

EDWARD PAYSON

How priceless is your unfailing love, O God! You give [us] drink from
your river of delights. For with you is the fountain of life;
in your light we see light.

PSALM 36:7-9 NIV

*W*hen God has become our shepherd, our refuge, our fortress,
then we can reach out to Him in the midst of a broken world
and feel at home while still on the way.

HENRI J. M. NOUWEN

I've loved you the way my Father has loved me.
Make yourselves at home in my love.

JOHN 15:9 MSG

There are times, and there will be times, when it will be absolutely clear that only God's grace keeps us from falling apart; and even if we cannot hold on to Him, He will still hold on to us.

JOHANNES FACIUS

$\mathcal{T}$hose who live in the shelter of the Most High will find rest
in the shadow of the Almighty.... He will cover you with his feathers.
He will shelter you with his wings.
His faithful promises are your armor and protection.

PSALM 91:1, 4 NLT

*I*n physics...every action is met by an equal or an opposite one....
And yet, along comes this idea called Grace to upend all that
"as you reap, so you will sow" stuff. Grace defies reason and logic.
Love interrupts, if you like, the consequences of your actions,
which...is very good news indeed.

BONO

The LORD is compassionate and gracious,
slow to anger, abounding in love.

PSALM 103:8 NIV

*L*ook deep within yourself and recognize what brings life and grace into your heart. It is this that can be shared with those around you. You are loved by God. This is an inspiration to love.

CHRISTOPHER DE VINCK

The Lord _appeared to us...saying:_ "I have loved you with an everlasting love; I have drawn you with unfailing kindness."

JEREMIAH 31:3 NIV

Throughout biblical history, we see the thread of God's grace toward us. Like the melodic theme of a symphonic masterpiece, it recurs in variations, singing over us, weaving together the story of God's love for His people.

MICHAEL NEALE

For the Lord your God is living among you.... He will take delight in you with gladness. With his love, he will calm all your fears. He will rejoice over you with joyful songs.

ZEPHANIAH 3:17 NLT

Ellie Claire™ Gift & Paper Corp.
Minneapolis, MN 55378
www.ellieclaire.com

Amazing Grace: My Stories, My Faith, My Life
© 2013 by Ellie Claire™ Gift & Paper Corp.

ISBN 978-1-60936-913-2

Stock or custom editions of Ellie Claire titles may be purchased in bulk
for educational, business, ministry, fundraising, or sales promotional use.
For information, please e-mail specialmarkets@summersidepress.com.

Compiled by Barbara Farmer
Cover and interior design by Greg Jackson | Thinkpen Design

Printed in China